Don't Call Me Elvis

And Other Poems

Gbanabom Hallowell

Sierra Leonean Writers Series

Don't Call Me Elvis
And Other Poems
Copyright © 2016 by Gbanabom Hallowell

ISBN: 978-99910-54-24-7

Sierra Leonean Writers Series

To the memory of
        Tom Cauuray,
                A tormented Sierra Leone poet

CONTENTS

DON'T CALL ME ELVIS, 1

Don't Call Me Elvis, 2
I'm Federal, 4
The Picture of Freddie Gray, 5
Zimmerman is Certainly Not Guilty, 6
Achebe Was Longer Than the Nile, 8
Road of the Roadless, 9
In the Name of Socrates, 10
One Hundred Lines for Nelson Mandela, 11
Love in the Time of Ebola, 16
What's in a Name?, 18
Elvis is in the Building, 20
The Wretched of the Sun, 21

A LITTLE AFTER DAWN, 22

In the Footwall, 23
Taste of the Day, 24
After Saturday Monday Will, 25
The End of the Road, 27
Democracy is Becoming, 29
Onward to the Sun We March, 31
The Only Right, 32
Bomaru, 34
The Next Time I Arrive at This Place, 36
There is the Incidental Love of the Man Who Comes, 38
A Fierce Thought is Swinging, 39

Inside of This Courageous Afternoon, 41

Under the Hour of the Time, 43

I Was Looking at You Looking at the Sea, 45

It's Official, 47

Citizen of the Past Where is Your Country?, 48

Animal Conscience, 50

One War is Over, 52

Afterwards Let Us Play War, 54

The Function of a Truth is the Dysfunction of a Lie, 56

I Come for a Drink, 57

"Why Did We Go to War?" ,60

You Have to Understand, 62

I Opened My Window in the Bottom of the Sea, 64

On a Normal Day I Can Never Think of War, 66

There Are Predicaments One Easily Leaves, 67

A Little After Dawn, 69

Can Someone Spare Me a Moment?, 71

Freetown, 73

And the Man Who Just Arrived, 74

Jokibu, 76

Yenga on My Mind, 78

At the Gates of Hell I Was Told, 81

When the Stone Picked Up a Life, 82

In Spite of My Resolve to Gather Myself in the Rain, 84

Looking Black in the Rain, 86

Your Father, 88

Come With Me, 92

A Bright Day Oozes Out of the Mouth of the Iguana, 93

The News at Nine, 95

Like the Trees of the Forest, 96

I Have Since Stopped Loving You With My Eyes, 97

WHEN SIERRA LEONE WAS A WOMAN

Nine and the Half, 99
A Kiss Could Have Saved the Day, 100
Love in the Smoke, 101
Before the Night Could Bloom, 102
Things Fall Apart, 103
Queen of the Lips, 104
Was That Why You Left By the Backdoor?, 105
The Pensive Mood of Desire, 106
Inside the Outside, 107
Under the Skin of Your Knife, 108
Your Beauty Moves Me, 109
The Brutal Language of Love, 110
Before The Evening, 111
The Journey of Love, 112
Tell Me Sia Leona, Tell Me Athens, 113
Between Two Mortalities, 114
A Song of No Free Rein 155
The Adolescent Woman, 116
Against Remembering, 117
These Drums Must Always Beat, 118
Salute at the Foot of up Gun, 199
One Night at Lumely Beach, 120
Bunce Island on my Mind, 121
Ferry me across River Rokel, 122
A River of Two Scarcies, 123
Earthworks at Maskpaidu, 124
Old Wharfs Steps, 125
Loveless at Lake Sonfon, 126

Amistad of the Sierra, 127

Approaching Freetown, 128

Anthem of De Ruyter, 129

Malaneh, 130

The Martello Tower in the Sierra, 131

Someone had to Love Madam Yoko, 132

The Economic Mind of Bai Bureh, 133

Gbanka of Yoni, 134

Kai Londo of Kailahun, 135

Confession of Sia Leona's Colonizer, 136

I.T.A of Wallace Johnson, Come forth, 137

King Kama Dumbuya, 138

Yulisa, 139

Death in the Family, 142

The Vanity of a Lifespan, 143

In The Pen Dense, 145

Re Pour Bleak, 146

Demo Crack Trick, 147

Half Ricka, 148

By Bull, 149

Hint Her Land, 150

When Sierra Leone Was a Woman, 151

Don't Call Me Elvis

DON'T CALL ME ELVIS

For several years, with a colonial tendency,
A desperate guitar has been eating into my fingers,
Licking the cracked barrels of my oily mouth
To smoothen the oesophagus of its strangled notes,
Twisting white voice into black sound—cannot
It be said that such an ambition has blood in mind?

It came from a rough dream, tumbling unto my feverish
Soul, bringing along all the elements called its conquerors
And the sadness of its Bible, placed between its Sunday palms;
Cord after cord, the leading lamps rattled in their flames while
The raging fires went ahead of themselves as fraudulent gold—
Cannot it be said that such an entrance prepares for no exit?

In the first track of its labyrinth, several musings tried to
Compose into a single song, coming toward me
As a pound of my own flesh with my blood
Dripping from the wild uncontrollable strings
Metallic, concrete, balls of blood, hesitating, and then springing
From the strings, like a frog, aiming for green landing—
Cannot it be said that such a flight of blood
Does not survive its own fire?

The guitar breathed with animal severity; it had to drop a name
On my mind in the form of a singing note; but my African

Forest was full of sudden hearts, beating
On the knees of the *griot,* leaping in flames
Emitting from the apexes of the eye of the land
Under the cherubim of the daily cocoa leaves
That was warming my name in its deep palms—
Cannot it be said that such is *Africare?*

In the end, the guitar sang me a familiar song,
Cuing to the drums of the *poro* beats.
As the Raka leaped into my face, my eyes
Opened itself to the naming mirror,
Then, Pa Manchiar uttered,
And like the silent breath of an opening bud,
The wind brought forth the primordial resolve,
Gbanabom—cannot it be said that such a resolve
Requires me to say, *don't call me Elvis?*

I'M FEDERAL

These persistent vigils have murdered
All the ancient republics, and most amazingly,
All the languages have lost their words, the
Vowels are torn into two. I live only with
The consonants; so, I'm federal, like a bomb
Placed in a dark place, I'm federal, like a book
That refuses to open its nose. For lack
Of vowels, I stagger in my courage, unable
To read the lips of the linguist who comes
In robes to donate words to my mouth.
Ten shillings a vigil, I am the slave pinned
To the door, a belly full of consonants,
I watch all the vowels in communist gowns
But I dare not leave the door, inside
Of which I have refused to observe the vigil
After being named Elvis by the colonial outsider

THE PICTURE OF FREDDIE GRAY

Basil Hallward did not know Baltimore
Until he became an American—by which
Time he had murdered Dorian Gray in flesh
Wrapping his soul in a paint of eternal paper.
Oscar is only a Wilde messenger
And so am I, feeling grey in my black skin.
The evergreen war of black and white,
Of police artists and black crimes,
Of blackened pots and cooked white rice,
Of white pieces of chalk and blackboards

ZIMMERMAN IS CERTAINLY NOT GUILTY

Zimmerman is not guilty, his gun is.
The quick nozzle of American neighborhood
Simply fed the intruding black Christ
The cup of his own black life. Zimmerman,
A wanna-be cop proved that he loved the Neighborhood
More than he loved the neighbor,
Less than his self-consciousness:
In this experimental American justice system,
Zimmerman is a bestseller epic novel,
The fierce Genre of Hollywood.
George Zimmerman judged for himself the quick
Blackness of the fierce dark brother.

Briefed like a truly American cop,
Zimmerman is cloned in blue eyes.
The venomous blood on the broken panes,
That never was there,
On the beagonvillia, that never was there,
On the patio, that never was there, in the lawn,
That never was there—and the black shadow
Of Trayvon Martin bringing back the briefing:
"This guy looks like he's up to no good,
Or he's on drugs or something. It's raining,
And he's just walking around,

Looking about and looking at the houses."
So that all black folks
When they hear of the death of Trayvon Martin
Will honor the intermediate range
Between the confederation and the cemetery
Of black freedom trapped in Martin and Malcolm.
This liberty fought for by my father
Who suffered through the Atlantic
Killed Trayvon in the neighborhood
Of this celebrated American freedom.

Dear Trayvon Martin,
Black as I am, even in Africa, I too I'm restricted.
Kleinfotein holds a South African gun to my head
This 95th birthday of Nelson Mandela.
I cannot go through that German town
Protected by the bust of Hendrik Verwoerd
Without his grandchild sniffing my blood
With his multiracial nostrils, O Adam O Eve!

ACHEBE WAS LONGER THAN THE NILE

On this Africa I lean
While mourning Chinua Achebe
My instant sagacity and the peanut
On its stem deafen the tongue-taste
Oil palm proverbs on the towel
Smartens the Igbo smell
Broom of languages
Nile to Nile, Zambezi to Zambezi
The mother has become death
At the door of the kinsman

Achebe, your eyes are closing before Idoto
And the belch of the dead emits
From the stone-head of Okigbo
Because of you I am my own Biafra
And I am my own Nigeria
Africa was another country
Another country was Africa
Achebe *Kwenu*, Achebe *Kwenu*
Can I not rename my Africa,
Can I not refer to the *Aprica* of Africa?

ROAD OF THE ROADLESS

Cover my head with the shawl of the dead
O apotropaic calabash
And set me on the terra-cotta
Journey on the edges of the living world
Where the sea stitches with the sky
Veridical of my kola-nut desire
I long for the embrace of my exiled lover
I long to touch the rattling beads round her waist
And to scroll my hand on the memory of our past
Bring back to me the divine gnosis
The tablet of the exodus
That I can recall the primordial mind of my lover
O calabash set me forth on a journey of hope
So that I can develop the muscles of the Atlantic
And with the gulosity of Atlas embrace my lover!

IN THE NAME OF SOCRATES

In the name of Socrates, I ask for a political dialogue
Between you and the longest
Hair standing tall on your head
Look into the eyes of your eyes of fetishism
And speak truth to your leadership
Ask yourself to lower your eyes
Below the bottom of your ego
And point your fingers toward your shadow
When your anger runs out
Walk slowly on the tight rope of your severity
And share any new experience
With the longest hair on your head

The expression "I" defies the mathematics of zero
On the bed of the table lies the body of an alien algebra

ONE HUNDRED LINES FOR NELSON MANDELA

Madiba Rolihlahla!
How difficult to write a poem on the screen
Where I have known him all his life—this Madiba essence.
I know my television is a ball of resurrection
But first I have to see him die, to see his eyes
Close effortlessly, taking in all the verdant agony,
All the assets of pain in one big gulp.
Until his death the screen would not show.
The flight disappears in the clouds, in the white
Ceremony of the clouds; so, even with the launching
Of the new satellite there will always be more
Creations than 46664 can separate itself
From the instant the moment of the domestic screen.
Speaking of which I dare not speak of channels
Until he shall return in motion media to hammer
Home the saints that he said he never was among;
Or to pick up the brown dress of his usual mind;
Or to see to it that what he said was true, that he would
Come again and still the figment would be in the square.
He saw a slave across the breasts of his finality
By which time his eyes were shutting down.
The concept of his own desire, to die, just as he had
Lived, not trusting the saints who now gather to bury him.
Beside the eventual moment, the mortal breath
He knew all too well coming to him like a tormenting Bible.

11

This time he was not prepared to die if his jaws had not
Fallen below his expectation, if his eye bags had not
Hidden from him the severity of seeing his painful

Face on TV even when he had left all his anger and
His prison clothes and his cost-effective soul behind, taking
Only his innocent mind, hoping to make it a citizen of the world.
They will come from Europe where they wanted him dead,
Where Thatcher grew up to know him as a terrorist;
From the United States where he preceded Osama
As the bean leavened with a jingoistic dignity under
The knife, even long after the butcher had perished.
But they will come and in them he will return again and again.
In his sleep he heard his mourners say there shall no longer
Be a Mandela, but do they not know that what they utter
Was a creativity of truth, that what they mourn does not
Die before it is born? Did they not watch the funeral
Service of Christ in the news on TV when his tree
Tied him to his own composure? Christ was on the BBC.

Steve Biko died in the ring, Mandela died in the pew.
Mandela was a humble man, he certainly knew who the saint was,
Where that saint took the blows when they reigned from white
Heavens; Biko took them in the ring; it was in the ring he took
The blows until he was able to strike one single blow.

How sad, saints don't die on TV screens.
Mandela is the kind of man you would be glad you were wrong
About when you thought he should have come out of prison
With at least a drug of anger? How could he not have had
A Kevorkian doctor whether black, Indian or even white
At a time when an Indian boasted about being his lawyer
In the ample Ghandian style? Someone is hurting history.
Can one ever say R.I.P. to the children of the screen
When their demise is always nothing more than a digital
Hitch? And now here we are, in the sorrow of our own

Christmas, at a time the dead should be left to bury their own
Dead, we are making Christ as imaginary as he was
In that crowded Jerusalem looking over an impossible dawn.
I have a ceremonial heart I wear for those who touch
My soul in ways that a memory stick cannot remember.
It is in no way ritualistic that I should cross both
My hands across my chest when mourning Mandela.
My friends would tell you that I had placed my right hand
On my chest when my father lost his earthly September this year.
This man who died one thousand times before his death
Shamed the notorious echo of that grey passage full of cobwebs.
It had come only when Mandela beckoned to it,
To shut its rage and the ego on its branded shoulders.
In the end Mandela now lives more alive than dead

We, his offspring will remain proud of only one of two phases
The living phase, which has the power of ascendancy.
Primordial man, known for his long walk to freedom,
The road, for that matter, any road must beware of its winding
Path, its secrecy and of the secrecy of its rurally minded urbanity.
In Madiba, heaven and earth have passed away, they have passed
Away with the vanity of their own blood, their own tears and
Their own sweats in the singular sacrifice of the painful Zulu,
Brother of the Gold Coast, of African Athens built on the Sierra
Overlooking the Rokel that feeds into the faithful Atlantic,
Brother of the Ivory, brother of the Nile, brother of the Zambezi
And of the Malagasy resolve, brother of the Tanganyika,
Of the Sahara where the Nubian thirsted for his intervention,
Of the rainforest, brother of the everglades, the hunger rice farm
Of the ubiquitous African freedom, of the *Ethiopic* Afrika.
When he stood before the Kangaroo brothers vying to fight

Against their Kangaroo philosophy, wrapped around his rope
He killed their spirits by offering them his throat and his neck;
What he stood for he was prepared to die for. It was then
That it occurred to us that it was him who had cut their
Throats and broken their necks, all in one Kangaroo hour.
In opening, I spoke about how difficult it was to write a poem
Regarding one whose life took a ninety-fifth turn of event.

You come as July 18, the seventh essence of our annual renewal
The philosophy you died for—the English will seal their ubiquity
By giving the dictionary meaning of Mandela in the contrastive
Black light that made it clear, even at night the sky remains blue,
And the world remains safe for people of a rainbow heart!

LOVE IN THE TIME OF EBOLA

The sorrow brothers abroad fear that at home
We are dropping dead like tornado mangoes,
Green with tears. The sorrow sisters fear that at home
We are dropping dead like tornado mangoes,
Green with tears. The Diaspora in tears, feeding on
The painful memory of the war still under our soles,
Long ago in another memory, another brambly--
Yesterday returns tomorrow in viral defiance
Shrouded in the winter of everyone's discontent.

They call us every day from abroad, their phones
Taking over the deserted skies that have sunken
All the aeroplanes in the muscles of the black African
Clouds; they call us to hear that we have all not died
In one viral drop; we wait; we hope. Not all white people
Have stopped flying into us and out of us. God is white
And he flies like a black bird over us, speaking in tongues
Not found in Quranic or Biblical books, not in Holy water
or *Surah* water, but in the deeply black African resolve.

There are two cups to be taken away from us because
We cannot drink them both. The cup of us dying
Like beasts besides our tired Bibles and our tired Qurans,
And the cup of our Diaspora brothers and sisters
Writhing in cold countries, dying besides themselves

Because we die at home blatantly in disregard of their broken
Hearts and their hospitalizing distances
Creeping into their mileages and mileages of helplessness;

O Diaspora O Africa, shall we forever be in tears,
Perishing both at home and abroad, when,
Wherever we are we shout the loudest to God?

WHAT'S IN A NAME?

Elvis your name is on the wrong
Perimeter; my mother cannot utter you,
Cannot rectify the blue eyed black son
With his sudden cold nose
Walking toward the cathedral
Voltage, hands akimbo,
Dumb as the sea, hearing only its own
Academic raging
Drowning itself in suicidal hope,
That rings of virgins
Shall touch the face of his path,
Imaginary though it is both in its wetness
And in its dryness.

When a name is born vampires
Crawl over its mane
To determine its association in the building.
Now here I am in strange four walls
With legs of water
Carrying a name in the place where
There already was one,
With all its indigenous carnivals
Speaking in professorial drums,
Of a restless name,
Calling to itself to answer in a rattling echo.

18

Mama, I am up from the piano,
And I'm looking to dance
With you, to retrace the loamy
Beats you played me in the Womb;
The calculated rhythm of your indigenous
Pain had long figured out
That Gbanabom shall be his own poet,
His own singer, here in this familiar perimeter!

ELVIS IS IN THE BUILDING

This building I am familiar
With has no inside,
No level of wind cuts its edges
In that rear space
Reserved for sons of the urgent
Breasts, so how come
Elvis, of unfathomable
Distance, can stand on his two
Legs with all his esoteric clarity,
To announce himself as the man through
Whom all other men have become men?

Or did someone announce the descent
From the blue anger of the clouds
In a soul of white gown, and a guitar
Of night singing a song strange to our ears?
Does it not bother the brothers that a whole
Winter came through this region
Without us knowing about it?
I do not know the longings
Of this desperate guitar;
What African aura its fire wants
To go through to seek the waters of my night?
On the platform of what African dream
Does this American identity want to possess my soul?

20

THE WRETCHED OF THE SEA

Water and blood drink each other in 700 persons
Between Libya and an Italian strip; the *Mare Nostrum*
Drowns the wretched each mundane death.
The bellicose sea belch the black mundane man
As he hiccups on his conscience besides his black woman,
In the vain journey on the raft of Medusa.
There is the future urchin with a sore tasty to the mangy dog.
Africa, each bite is followed by a sting, by a thorn.

Several hundreds of Africans die in the Mediterranean,
In the wicked sea while sailing the *Mare Liberum* which once
Brought, through that same death trap, the Black Plague,
Having dominion over black souls, rippled dark
Spirits, seeking the remnants of Eden, the artificial
Garden built where there was no Eden. Dead
Is the sea, dead in the conscience of Cain; in the
Innocence of an African Abel clutching burnt sacrifices.

Habitual weekend bodies float black in sea coasts
After the deluge of human bondage. Africa, the sea
Eats your children who seek to be volunteer slaves.
Mothers of these roaming cadavers search your womb,
Are there any more children left to tender the garden?
The boarders of Algeria and Libya are feeding the sea
With your children ahead of their corpses as they head
For Europe in shrouds, O this lugubrious journey!

A Little After Dawn

IN THE FOOTWALL

In the footwall
a decade
lingers
in mineral sore throats,
even the night cannot sleep.

I have become
a souvenir
unto the
souvenir of war
and now
the big road
denies me a passage
backward into my spirit body,
forward into my physical soul.

To the dusty body
of my verses follow me,
to live within the four walls
of my imageries and metaphors,
to look me up in my miserable *Bambakayaka*[1].

---

[1] *A term developed within the last ten years in Sierra Leone to describe life in prison. Its etymological origin is uncertain.*

TASTE THE DAY

Taste the day
When it is ending on your tongue
And with your nose
Follow your own eyes
That behold it.

Embrace the night
Oozing from under the hill,
Afterwards,
Celebrate your Freetown
In the middle
Of your chest.

Afterwards, calm down
Like the unborn sea;
And with sudden suddenness
Bellow like the temporary
Muscle of the raging ocean
For the country in your head.

AFTER SATURDAY MONDAY WILL

After Saturday Monday will
take over. After the train goes down
the blood pressure of the night will upset
the moon, and the moon will pour over Freetown,
over the silent river that runs into the wild sea;
after the holidays the schools will remain shut
and all the school children will run to the river
to watch their teachers drown.

After the road another road will spring in the forest
but will abort in the narrow path of the politicians
who have still not agreed on the right spelling
of Freetown with the capitalization
of the Province of Freedom.

After my death another man will die, and
another too will die even also on the eve of my death;
but before all of these happen
there has to have been created a Saturday
and then a Monday between two Sundays and then a long
reason should follow as to why we will
never want to spring into these days ordinarily like roads.

After a term of office a leader
shall fall into our trap just like we fell

25

into his trap five years ago. We shall return
his favor on a day that he can remember
as Saturday which shall precede Monday
with all its serious morning mood.

After the terms of reference are drafted
the soldier will fidget his rifle while a snake
rattles in his mind. He will be sternly questioned
by his platoon commander but he would
merely giggle and suddenly think
about *Bambakayaka* where his peers
are languishing.

After the day is over the accompanying night will
call it a day—only the blackness will
traverse the earth in boots drunk and reckless
and with a friend in hand the city too can call it a day.

THE END OF THE ROAD

The end of the road
ends when it ends,
when the goer returns a right foot
a step backwards and when the goer refuses
to bring a left foot a step forward.
Perennial partner, O road the goer wants
to walk away from you to allow
you to continue your journey alone
into the woods, into the mind of the big
hole that you came from long ago.

Even I have always enjoyed our conversations
struck when I first came upon you
with a beer in my hand and the left over
of an old lover who committed suicide
in my troubled heart. Your ubiquitous memory
peels off like a banana and the slippery
narrative of your back runs the journey along.
I am susceptible to your cavernous friendship,
to your lying tongue that scoops into horizontal
history, bringing it right into my vertical emptiness.

Now, when this day is over, I would still like
to have you in memory, granted as life to the frame
of the body of man—you never ever go away anyhow

since you only always rise and fall or as the academic
brother would say—you increase and occupy yourself—
it is this power that I see the five or six million people

whom I call countrymen and countrywomen exploit
every day to survive, to live and to die;
to follow after their clean and dirty minds,
to lower and to lift themselves, but not a flower for you.

On every sad day I imagine that if within your secret
anger you suddenly decide to retreat into yourself, away
from my Sierra Leonean sorrow, pulling your distant support
from among the hills of Koinadugu, your watery presence
from Bonthe, your fingernails from the tight city of Freetown,
your terracotta surge from the pits of Kono, your cold silence
from the cacao beds of Kailahun, your tentative curves
from the womb of Magburaka, your patient crawling from the
sore soul of Yenga, that would be for me the end of the road.

DEMOCRACY IS BECOMING

Democracy is becoming
a whirlwind
under the skirt of an old
lady because
particles
have gone into its eye;
into
the corner of the eyes' eye,
also into its vision,
the eye of its vision—and
the little ladies
keeping company
on
the dirt road
where the terracotta mind
ends
have fallen into a hysteria,
laughing
their sides out.
Democracy is a hot cocoa
in the hat of an old
drunkard
who picks his steps
in the grassland;
a confederation

of used pants and
shattered lipstick bottles;
of old tobacco pipes and
broken shoes.
Democracy
breezes
its
fingers
on
the
sorrows
of
the
world like a smooth ride.

ONWARD TO THE SUN WE MARCH

Onward to the sun we march
Onward to the moon they march
We hold our heads above fallen rain
They follow their shadows to the ground to sleep
In their consciences
In their own thoughts
It is raining spontaneously
Reigning between two seasons
A throne of clouds changes in the air
And a king waits under like a pebble

THE ONLY RIGHT

The only right
I have sworn to die for is yours.
While I can negotiate mine with the devil
I do not find it worth dying for. In fact, I shout
about mine merely because I see yours
in a global accident—a drenched soul in this vehicle,
a tabernacle in the region of this new Mecca,
a new city housing ancient people all living
in Rights Street with dictionaries of foreign words
and unspoken languages, seeking to patch a Babel,
seeking to speak for the people with no language
to call their own—this I have vowed to die for
with a flute in hand and a hand on the legendary bone.

As well as hope, man thrives on anything right,
any chair crossed to the right of a table with
a lamp stood on the right end of the top, and the joint
end of my own quality of life will die for your singular
right, and the rights you don't even care to number
on your smiling lip—I will die for those too,
for the forceful bone stuck out of the young mind
and left to run like blood on the light skin
of a child born in the middle of war;
your right has consumed my heart
and so I stand in the middle of my experience

to throw this little javelin with the power
of my left hand, a hand on the legendary bone.
This affair is going to occupy all my time,
that of giving up my life for your right
and the other perimeters of your right
to be a leaf or the bark of a tree or the moment
in the body of the wind hurrying to spread
across the landscape of the endless West African
desert, or for that matter any known desert
in the human memory.

I have travelled through rifles
to come for your right hand and with
my perpetual left handedness I lead you across
the Island of your own confidence,
through this Sierra Leonean illusion
brought about by Portuguese pretense—
forgive my left hand.

BOMARU

For Abu, my younger brother, KIA

Bomaru
lies between the two eyes of the future,
on the pale memory of a broken war
fought in the empty landscape of the Sierra.
And after all of that archaic water crossing
a dog is making love to another dog on the spot
where executive bombs dropped,
shaking the laughter of Pythagorean
men behind the wheels of war.
Two dogs,
a road
on a road
that lions and tigers once fled from.
Ten years later Bomaru exists without evidence.
Bomaru is as Bomaru was: no pound of evidence,
only the humid history of footsteps shown in the dark
skies of its evening.

The yellow mind of Bomaru
rises and sets with the sun and the large
smoke in the center of the town's affair
illuminates forgetting. Anyone can buy
or accept a drink in wooden cups and pretend glasses.
Ugly rifles and their bullets play festivals
around the tireless ankles of the young.

No one knew not that when Bomaru was Bomaru
the town went down on its knees in the soul
of the nine lives of the coward,
taking possession
of this boarder town
in all its blue perimeter;
but today the reiverside guerillas have looked
into the new mirror behind of which
are joyous girls of the other Bomaru.
Where two dogs
delight afterschool children
on the road that lions and tigers once fled from.

THE NEXT TIME I ARRIVE AT THIS PLACE

The next time I arrive at this place,
at this same place where your shadow interacts with mine,
I shall require of you to rise above your eyes
so that mine can find some time to rest as we converse.

This brings me to the next thigh bone between our two distances
and the lateral day pushing you to a fraudulent calendar month
close to my guarded November, close to a windfall
that speaks of the time and time erected between our friendship.

Eight hours have gone by since we gathered here to converse,
to dig inside the dialogue that is deafening our ears,
to believe that white is black in the desert,
to remember that yesterday existed only in foreign lands.

Sonorous whispers fall from the sky,
all in eight hours before the anticipated Christmas
during which we are taught to believe that white is black on desert
before the Easter arrives with its own kind of Christmas.

Eight Sierra Leonean hours spent back to back
believing that colors disfigure in the desert,
believing that you are only meant to be my brother
in a desert full of snout of snout and of slippery people.

Eight immediate hours have gone by between us
and four more circulate the epicenter of our conversation
waiting to consume the animals we have brought
for the sacrifice to seize the mind of the desert.

In the name of the father and of the son
and of the whole globe I demand my life back
free of deserts and of cubic hours,
free of white that turns black and of black that turns white.

Octagonal country, I sit beside myself on the wounded edges
of your mind trying to make sense of our tribal friendship
through the sacrificial beast tethered to our legs;
woman, come to us as a mother.

Woman, mother of two brothers
my shadow and I are keeping vigil in your eight
hours of labor and in your octagonal bosom;
bring forth a brother before I die of loneliness.

THERE IS THE INCIDENTAL LOVE
OF THE MAN WHO COMES

There is the incidental love of the man who comes
And the quick anger of the man who goes.
Between them are the bodies of trees with souls.
There is the darkness that divides them into love and hate
And always a little child coming from the body of a woman.

There is a woman inside of a man,
Instantly the woman levels the man into children.
There is an argument inside of a god,
Instantly the god goes mute.
There is a liquid inside the water,
Instantly a tributary drowns into the ocean.

A lame moment is coming my way;
And in readiness I clutch my beer between my breasts.
A breath comes out of my beer bottle and mingles with mine.
Throat to throat I wait for the lame authority of the moment;
I turn into a second, into a minute and into the large
Hour of a clock.

A FIERCE THOUGHT IS SWINGING

A fierce thought is swinging
around the fire of the sun, the hot
burning moment of the entire sun, hanging
on the rope of a waist.

A national day is celebrating itself today
even though it is not in the memory of citizens;
but when this day shall have finished celebrating
the six hundred people who saw Mabayla for the one last
time in their lives shall address the afternoon accordion .

I am in the center of this shame because my shoes
cannot go off my feet to follow after the strictness
of the clock and the enormous fire in the middle of the sun.

I have skidded from the shoulders of the earth
to follow this day from the eyes of the unexpected Mabayla
to see the ventilating energy pouring from the fire of the sun,
the determined cemetery with its human tenderness.

Pity for the dumb trees unable to identify history
and for the river unable to reject the yesterday corpses
and for the hills hunching every moment with madness
and for a day like this celebrated in the field of smoke.

I am in the rain celebrating the day I don't see in the day;
a cold logic is swarming in the air in shrouds
and a terracotta mind is in the blue of shape, stubbornly
anticipating a Mabayla moment to throw back to the present.

A big day is shrinking before my eyes and aiming for the nose
of a soul in this Mabayla, city of the regent pain; opaque man
opaque town opaque logic and opaque, a cemetery of celebration.

Mabayla, erect your collar on your imaginary
sentimentality and pose for the accolade of the silence
to give power to this day, your day between no day.
Who will deny you the silence of your own smile?
Who will? Who will? Who will?

INSIDE OF THIS COURAGEOUS AFTERNOON

Inside of this courageous afternoon
when the south goes into its southernmost self
and the prominence of the eye rests on an object,
the little truth tells itself in defiance of the big truth;
and the colony claims its history
in this known Bunumbu, in this lovely remembering
of the alternate self; of the self, first known in the unknown,
suddenly coming to shore from abroad on broad shoulders.

A naked night passes blindly burning by a degree of thought,
taking along it the pride of the sinful children
all in a century, running through a gorgeous moment
with a substantial desire to beget me in this land
through the night beds of *pehwabu*[2]
and the tormented nights of the frogs eventually afflict
the earth in my being, in my reasonable desire
to be a being in defiance of obligation breathed in me.

Flesh comes on its own accord to every unconscious object
and in that moment as I get scared by reality
I become a child of day and a child of noon
in between a morning journeying with its still flowers
ever afraid to dare a kiss to the hating sun.
I store myself a name in boxes

---

[2] *Mende expression for a large open apartment for elderly women in-mates*

41

so that I can use it to answer to anyone who calls
on me to use the white bowl to drink the waters of my thirst.

This universal face of Bunumbu sought my father out
to seek me, to drag me into its corset, into the figure
of its mathematics. A Bunumbu seen only through a Monday
spectacle, laid a hand on the morning spirit of the national river,
sending only its waters of showers this end of my stream
with its local soap suds forming and sinking
into my innocent eyes full of pepper wisdom
as the dutiful hand of the women of the *pehwabu* elbows on.

This afternoon my father sits in the front house looking
at another afternoon, that one that brought him to Bunumbu
when he himself was too young to decide whether to move
his right hand or his left hand from
Besides his ribs to his bosoms,
from between his thoughts to his miracle bones, from across
his sad face to his white teeth, from among his fingers to his
crowded toes; and when finally he leans back on the chair
thinking—Bunumbu scared him with a gift
wrapped in a woman's mind.

UNDER THE HOUR OF THE TIME

Under the hour of the time
many skies scurry searching for a posthumous
love in a most fundamental temperament;
in the pillars of clouds that fight back making faces.
The Sierra is in those clouds close to Ethiopia,
holding hands with people of the Sahara!

love in the sky, fly for its blue eyes
love in the sea, swim for its water
love on the ground, reach for its dirt
love between two freedoms, celebrate it.

Always on the road a man is walking between
two women; always on the road a woman
is walking between two men

The day is in love with the night;
the sky is in love with the sea; and the ground
is in love with itself.

On the road war is searching for love. Two people
in conflict running against each other with machetes
are searching for love. The drunkard enters the bar
seeking love on the counter; the sleeping toddler

43

is dreaming of love on his thin mat. The hungry man
and the mangy dog have made way for each other
under the cotton tree waiting for love to go their way.

There are of course situations in which love is hate—
in those situations everything stands still—not even
the door has the potential of going into itself. When
the bird falls from the sky and the kite unable to take off
love is in total hate—even hating itself.

I who talk of love knows no loving. The other
day Yandama urged me to go through a woman's
mind to find plenty of love; but all I found
in that mind was a giant shadow holding a touch searching
for something. I tried going through my own mind—
there was a nervous woman staring at a rattling snake.

I WAS LOOKING AT YOU LOOKING AT THE SEA

for Sarah Bomkampre

I was looking at you looking at the sea
and I saw the sea in you and you in the sea
and then I saw the sea instead of you
and you instead of the sea
and I saw nothing instead of you
and I saw nothing instead of the sea
and the sea saw me looking at the sea
and you saw me looking at you
and the sea and you saw me looking at nothing
and I saw you and the sea looking at me
and I saw you between the two waves of the sea
and I saw the sea between the two flames of your you
and I saw the highest muscle of the sea wrapped around you
and I saw your brightest flame lighting up the body of the sea
and I saw the sea stitched with the rain that dropped on it
and I saw you stitched with the soul that dropped on you
and I saw nothing between the sea and me
and I saw nothing between you and me
and I saw a hand between the sea and you
and I saw you between a hand and the sea
and I saw the sea between a hand and you
and I saw exuberance between the eye of the sea and your presence
and I saw a dancing canoe on the edge of your eyes
and you saw my pupils dancing to the silence of the canoe
and I took your hand between two resistances

and I saw the sea clung to your rising waist
and I left your hand and reached for that of the water
and I saw that where there was a hand a muscle had frozen
and I stepped beside your ego and that of the sea
and I remembered that the sea had no water
and I also remembered that you had no sex
and I saw a mirage in the middle of your doubt
and I saw a doubt in the middle of the mirage of the sea
and I saw a sea that was nearly not a sea by itself
and I saw a you nearly not a you by yourself
and I saw the sea reaching for a cup of water in the clouds
and I saw you reaching for a virginity in the valley of trees
and I saw the sea returning to its own sea
and I saw you picking yourself from the back of the receding sea
and I saw neither you nor the sea in my eyes

IT IS OFFICIAL

It is official
My death has been ticked in the book
And the announcement is made in the clouds
So it now means that I am officially now an angel
With wings to fly to places wherever God wants me to.

Henceforth, I should look out for my cloud in nine clouds
I should look for a fire in the tertiary cloud
The world will come under the photographer's stillness
And all the people will pause forever.

After my death everything else dies
The fire in the cloud dies, and the nine clouds too
Only one living thing writhes on the ground forever—
My Hope.

CITIZEN OF THE PAST WHERE IS YOUR COUNTRY?

Citizen of the past where is your country
or your nationality? Has your corpse figured out
the lanes in your drained blood?
Was it your country that fell from the sky
bringing along all the nine clouds
of that sad man sitting in silence in the moon?
Or was it your country that fled in front of the black sea
taking along its cowardice in its two hands?
Why do you approach us from the back of your past
to tell about all the things you carry in your two hands,
all that metal window oversized in your own understanding?
Can the day become exactly the sun?
Or can the sun boast of being the creator of the day?
What was ordinary yesterday that is extraordinary
today? What lines crossed your palms
yesterday that has abandoned its own road?
In what generation did you take
your own road before you lost knowledge
of your citizenry or that nationality
you shout about in the present time
even though you know not in what continent you belong?
Are you a child of my mother? In which of her pain
did you arrive in? Was it the pain in her thighbone
or that of the ankle that stretched with trinkets?
Was it the pain that brought forth Siamese

in the double conscience of a valley?
Does your country have rocks?

Does it boast of fossils of the rocks?
How vigorous was your love
that your country should fall away from your hands
and move away from the map of your head?
At the end of this moment where will
your bones lie? What country will
keep you for the return of the river you have lost
in your head? Why is it necessary that you
speak to a poet whose citizenry is lost in verse?
Does a country deserve a country to keep the citizen?

ANIMAL CONSCIENCE

Animal conscience—
not *humanimal* of the rifle membrane—
animal conscience of paper
soul and crispy desire;
on all four the road is tired of this brutality,
the rough breath of survival
and the saliva nudity in the green of jungle.

A conscience of claws and of paws,
hunger is in the eyes and in the quick
nostrils; so it is that the jungle shivers
under its own sensitivity.

In the place of brief days the nights
embrace the immortal thirst of the sweat
and even the sun can stealthily pass by
without the black leaves waking on the trees.

The prey hides in its own mouth
and rattles too in the same mouth,
under the same black leaves where
the predator waits in the back of the beyond
creeping through circles through
thick and thin generations.

Thunder clad jungle fire on the trees
as red river runs deep between the broken
garden of knowledge and truth,
touching the drugged conscience of the lion
and of the tiger, of the leopard and of the hyena
of the mamba and of the crocodile—
pretty dark and pretty bright, pretty dull
and pretty sharp, pretty dry and pretty wet—
the gruffer wind knows it all from the grassland
to the desert heartland where animals search for souls.

ONE WAR IS OVER

One war is over
and another one is picking up strength
among the experimental lettuces
in the backyard garden of nobody.
Six heroes are carried on the backs
of six other men feeding the latter on theories
plucked from the front garden of somebody.
Brother, it is raining on you so hard
and you cannot afford a shelter of leaves.
Which garden would grow hair
when the owner planted tomatoes?
Sister, wash your hands well and pluck
me some grapes near the tree by the house grave
and by the trees of the silent infant are oranges
good for the soul.
Brother, where is your garden
and what fruits fit the pocket of your mind?
Mangoes are too tall for a garden and
guavas don't do well in old people's mouth.
A loaf of bread is coming
directly from a grey garden
into my mouth,
what shall I do instantly?
Shall I run around in circles
or shall I boldly hide behind the end

of the butt of a gun and dare all the brutal
fruits of the unknown garden?

O fruit where is your fruit?
Your water inside your water?
where is the space left for your grown self?

Who was the human slave
sweating over your head
in human greed?

In what soil was your integrity sowed?
What secret was spoken in your ears
about your return? How many children
should you return with? Above all,
who resurrected you from the belly
of your faith?

AFTERWARDS LET US PLAY WAR

Afterwards let us play war
now that papa is cowardly sleeping on his opportunity.
When I shoot the string with my forefinger
die below your knees and spill your tongue on the floor
that mama shed a tear on last night for the brothers of the
revolution.

Lay your hand on the rock of my chest
and with a heavy heart I will take a bit of it
with my paper blade. Your uncle sitting
under the bitter tree will flee in his sleep
and we will laugh and laugh and laugh.

Let us cast an animal cloud in the village
and then hide in its reluctant wind;
Nanagbong, the village witch, will
go on her knees and pull back her quick
tongue to avoid a blade of blood on her awkward scar.

How do we get the villagers to run away
from everything? From their yesterday
and from their today, from their tomorrow
and from their dreams, from the end of war
to the beginning of war, and from themselves.

Let us build a rainbow across the village sky
and then hide behind its thunderclap
whose lightening would wire around
the house of exile and pull it to the village
and spill its caged anger in the square.

We are civilian fighters and our people must
acknowledge our sacrifices when we march
across town, when we bleed with patriotism;
we must be sung heroes of the years of the water,
we must be told *aha aha,* and be told again.

And again until we are sick of it and until we
laugh and laugh and laugh. Our sisters must
be let on us like dogs of war and together
we shall take the town in our hands, in our
hearts until peace returns from abroad.

THE FUNCTION OF A TRUTH
IS THE DYSFUNCTION OF A LIE

The function of a truth is the dysfunction of a lie.
From the bed of the tongue to the cave of the ear
Both carry equal weights;
Courageous decimal pieces and a long echo
Keep the road occupied on substances of the brain
Which experiences it all.

Anyone who tells a truth also tells a lie.
On the skin of only one tongue
Comes the many roads leading only to one place:
From the place of war to the place of war
Doesn't matter whether
It is a tributary of truths or of lies—
Because anyone who tells a truth also tells a lie.

I COME FOR A DRINK

I come for a drink
even if to a cup that is equally thirsty

I come for a walk
even if on a road tired of human steps

I come for a chat
even if to a friend who killed himself last night

I come for a fight
even if it's me against the world

I come to a woman
even if she embraces me apples in her eyes

I come to the beach
even if to feel her cold sands in my pants

I come to the night
even if I go missing inside its darkness

I come to myself
even if in the person of another

I come to the countryside
even if I arrive without a rainbow

I come to the end
even if I end up in the beginning

I tender my body to your ideas
even if the books walk awkwardly in thought

I come to my own congeniality
even if with an anger for the brother

I come as a number of ten
even if the mathematician cries in his sleep

I come to the drunkard
even if I lose my soberness to her

I come as an angel
even if my wings are no longer needed for the flight

I come to the teacher
even if I have lost my mind

I come to the fire
even if I have a knife between my teeth

I surrender my garment to the Christ
even if to commit suicide under his hopeful cross

"WHY DID WE GO TO WAR?"

"Why did we go to war?"

On this head argument is sleepless.
The hill is already grown into a pensive mountain
as rivulets against the numberless stumps tear the flesh.
Freetown is broken under Mount Aureol
between Mount Colony and Mount Independence.
The valley of Hamon-gog flows with dark memories
from the body of thoughts and from the thoughts of body,
and then the tears of lamentation flow like a river
and afterwards, the ultimate river itself flows like a river
washing away Mount Colony and Mount Independence.

The Sierra stands alone, cold,
outside its Freetown, outside its sadness and the sadness
of its capital, and on behalf of its own geography it sheds
a tear: why did we go to war?
To kill the son who put the man in the womb of the woman?
To talk to the brother who was busy buying his own
body in the market; to engage the sister who sat
in her conscience standing up?

Now the cage has walked up to us seeking after our bloody
conscience, and here we are unable to look under the bridge
of the cloud that yesterday sat over our immediate violence.

Who put a spectacle in the eyes of our dead,
seated outside, looking at us through the houses?

"Why did we go to war?"

I live between two pains—
between the pain of being Sierra Leonean
and the pain of being Sierra Leone.
My brother you too live between two pains—
between two private pains, the pain of going to war
and the pain of escaping the comradery of death.
I have given it all up as I sit beside myself
waiting for the rain.

YOU HAVE TO UNDERSTAND

You have to understand
Why every evening
I insist on spending some time
talking to the silence of the Wara Wara Mountain,
otherwise you will not know why I prefer the truth
of stone.

Who says mountains don't believe
in the God of speech?

Come closer and stand between
the mountain and me
if you must feel the stillness of my heart
on a day like this
when the day itself is gone.

I listen to the whirlwind in the inner stone
and the calmness of the black membrane
around the immortal rock.

Come and sit by me mother Sierra
come and sit by me children of the Sierra.

Tonight I take a ride across Africa
on the back of the Wara Wara.

A flight in my gaze, I sustain
in the center of the human acts of stone.

In short, I am engaging a philosopher
in the art of archeology,
in the terracotta history,
in the pigments of my geography.

I fulfill a calling under my cap, under my foot
ruined by the terracotta anger of the road.

How I wish I were a stone stuck to a stone
dark on the outside and unpredictable on the inside,
quiet on the outside and hunching on the inside,
naked on the outside and romantic on the inside.

I wish I were a stone's stone!

I OPENED MY WINDOW IN THE BOTTOM OF THE SEA

For John Conteh-Morgan

I opened my window in the bottom of the sea
to listen to those who speak of John Conteh-Morgan's
death. They speak of it in hendecasyllabic tones,
of this man called John Conteh-Morgan;
this man who together with me listened to the ranting of Vallejo,
and stood on his head all his life. This man to whom
the language of French sounded Italian.

When this poem is published John Conteh-Morgan
will show me the palms he took hot bread
into for the sake of my own belly which knows
hunger in linguistic energy. He will do this before
he celebrates his own death in the parlor of my tears
which itself is already holding the tears of other brother men.

It is painful to cry after other men have cried
unless one has to do so in rooms meant for the manchild.
My, to say I don't even know how to see birds across
the naked void of the sky, when all one needs to do
is to say "Mother, I have received the sun in the place of the moon
even when the gods are still thinking about the voided moon."

Let me hear it again, to know that it was John Conteh-Morgan
who died without preparing our minds. Let us know what
day he died, what season was it that deceived that day.

Let us know why we ourselves didn't die in the basic
truth of his death. Let us follow up on the brutal energy
of our own blindness that says to us the dead are asleep.

And finally, when the night comes upon me with its brutal
memory of love, I want to clutch my travelling pair of sandals
and swallow my ego while celebrating your lugubrious silence.

O shoes, the pair of you capable of taking me into your night,
into your own shadow, did the gods ask you to abide,
to kill a man whose window already opened in the sea?

ON A NORMAL DAY I CAN NEVER THINK OF WAR

On a normal day I can never think of war
On a normal day when the trees in the forests
Are threatened by a whirlwind I can only think of peace.

On a normal day I can never cry of hunger
On a normal day when my belly sees the skin of my back
I can only think of a sound sleep.

On a normal day I can never hate a brother
On a normal day when I find out that my wife is his fiancée
I can only think of the insurance company I didn't go to.

On a normal day I can never think of writing poetry
On a normal day, just on a normal day
I can only think of being a poet to myself and by myself.

THERE ARE PREDICAMENTS ONE EASILY LEAVES

There are predicaments one easily leaves
under the shoe whether one goes
for a walk or not, whether one
dies or not, whether one builds a house
or breaks it between two axe blows.

At the end of the war in this town
many of us still move about
with coffins strung on us;
and when they fall from us
we fall from them; and both
go on dying in the continuous past
buried as twin brothers by no one.

Here in this town we live on the ceremony
of hope believing that in dying
we shed the coffin of the war we did not die in.
Under his restless breath,
Tom Caurray, a brother poet
believed in his country more than he believed
in his country and for that reason
he lived all his life only in the country
of his country and one day he rolled
all the scrolls of his poems and died
on them leaning on their hendecasyllabic nonsense.

Other poets died after the war
I died after other poets died;
other poets died after I died,
and we were all buried in manuscripts
folded in coffins and dug in the throats of the Sierra.

After our deaths we made news,
we made news but not newspaper news,
we made news after the news.

A LITTLE AFTER DAWN

Against the universal thirst left behind by the war,
men, beasts and armored cars, broken on the wheels
seek to cross over the bridge at dawn and besides their
writhing souls licked the river leaves trembling beneath
the impatient apexes, the laminas, the blades and the trunk of God.

Tender water for the man, the beast and the machine;
listen to the man drinking from the tusk of the elephant
and to the rifle drinking from the lungs of the man;
listen to the eternal stone listening to the guttural
sun licking the backs of all three: machine, man and beast.

Licking his tears, the man weighs the confidence on his back
after sighting the afterblood of the machine, the afterblood
of the snake and the afterblood of the river they
drink from; the bullets and the bombs wash their hands clean after
passing through the mind of the cemetery to the ultimate

River to suffer from crossing to the new selves and from leaving
the old selves; the instant sagacity of the bridge is in the fresh
water uphill delayed by the hand of a rock and now
even the bridge is wearied and so too is its river under which
the water should settle in this city just from war.

With the passing of a smoke the river rises from the bridge
and from the anticipated water held at high places by a rock;
let the fatality of the bridge rise and disappear with the river
so that under the waiting air the coming water
cannot arrive with drowning ropes for any who come to drink.

Many tired souls are on their way to drink and to cross;
the rifle arrives leaving its butt behind it, the armored car
arrives, leaving its giant wheels stuck in the desert,
the animal arrives, leaving its beast behind it,
the man too arrives, leaving his hate behind him.

Finally when the rock lifts its hand from its own stone
the water gives up its calmness, hauling the rock
into the deep, heaving its own immensity on those that wait
to drink of its spring; under the sharp yellow looks of the bridge
new leaves begin to pick and the babies, on their oars, quench...

CAN SOMEONE SPARE ME A MOMENT?

Can someone spare me a moment?
I want to talk about the left
side of the right road. I want to talk about
the beautiful face of the ugly woman and about
the left toes of the right foot. I want to talk about
the dying ember of the sun and of the grey hair of the moon.

And I want to compare today to the day I envisaged
the night before when the tales of the final moon
left a big thought in my eyes. I want to be angry because
of the happiness pushing itself up my head. I want
to provide bread for the thief caught by a mob
and killed in the middle of his birthplace and I want
to provide a stone and a mirror
for each of the men who jumped on him.

I want to prove to the world that I do not exist and that
I began experiencing hunger even before I was born. I want
to jump from a cliff to the pages of a book about to be torn
by a three year old child to see how blood takes over
the clean pages of an innocent soul.

Whoever spares an hour shall spare a life.
Whoever spares a life shall spare a war.
Whoever spares a war shall spare another war.
Whoever spares another war shall spare a quarrel.

71

Exactly on a day no one can imagine
an imagination is going to turn into a complete day
with all its sun, moon,
rivers and flowing arguments
under the awkward boats of men forever condemned
to fish out drowned persons
from seas drowned in oceans, oceans always running away.

I want to run away like the ocean
and always return like a cloud;
and I want to be the unexpected rain falling
at an hour water already covers the earth. In such,
I want to go around unwanted. I want to be the one
never hooked by a question mark. I am running toward
an exclamation mark dangling on the rainforest tree.

FREETOWN

Freetown,
I want to run a thought
Across your face.
You are too free to be free,
And I'm worried about
How close you are to the sea.
Your pillow is getting too high
And too large on your thin bed.
Look how much the pillow case
Has ripped apart
And now when the clouds
Cry all your clothes go soaking wet.
You do not need that mosquito any more
To prick conscience into
The minds of the unmindful.

AND THE MAN WHO JUST ARRIVED

And the man who just arrived
asked the man who had arrived
earlier how it felt to arrive
into one's own loneliness?
And the other answered with a question
wanting to know how the man who had asked
about one arriving in one's loneliness
arrived in his own shoes?
The man who just arrived wanted to know
why when the earlier man arrived
his masculine energy
took the black road back and left him standing?
And then also, the man who just arrived
again wanted to know why when
the first man arrived he didn't arrive unto himself?
The man who arrived earlier wanted to know
whether the man who just arrived
knew why the road arrived with him at that point?
The road also wanted to know
why the point the two men stood to converse
was indeed a point of human arrival?

What arrival? Water departs around a domain
and the question leads without a mark nor the exclamation
with a mark. Who comes from a house of exile? Who walks

on a road leading to arrival, to exile or to a point of no return?
The lion is on the road and so is the snail—
all seeking an arrival. Seeking to achieve the closure—
the closure of a poem, the closure of an aged manuscript
peopled by characters who died before a publisher
could lay a hand on the mind of the writer. The lone
poet is on the road with a terracotta mind mindful
of the unpredictable enjambments of his poems—
the carver too is on the road smoothening
the crude hunger carvings hanging on the consciences
of the human arrivals at the point where the road left them.

The man who just arrived at the point
enquired of the man whom he met
whether his own arrival was the same as his departure.
The second man took three steps forward, turned
around and enquired of the man who just arrived
whether he was just going to stand there, arrived!

JOKIBU

Jokibu,
always under your fertility,
forever under your honor
my tiny conscience draws
closer to your forgotten
hand and my 1965 multiplies
my sorrow against a brow of blood
breeding the apprehension
of being proud of 2012;
but before your mirror
you contemplate only the son,
only the sun under
the fetus of the sky,
under the fetus of her own fetus,
hand of the under-mountain
pull me closer to the center,
to the area where your love blooms.
I have come home to come home.

I do not come to search
for myself; already there
is an argument up above
my head and you
made it clear that you wanted me
to be with you down below myself,

below the mountain
of my ego, below
whatever is below me.

Here I come then creeping
through the ages,
the vacuum between
us two, between
the creator and the created.

YENGA ON MY MIND

Yenga on my mind;
no longer at ease!
Sincerity has lost its ceremony
to the valley of death.
This purple hibiscus for which my mother
died a mother
now walks the Guinea road.
Where is that Sierra Leonean poet
who once bled the moon
to quench my thirst?
Yesterday the Cotton Tree madman
read from a deck of cards
the obvious pain of loss
exaggerated by the queen of hearts.
Being that the madman
too is a poet
I shall not cry over the water
that separates us.
This manual
calmness in my countrymen
over the affairs of Yenga
drinks my blood.
I long

for the momentary tongues
of Dawa, Kailondo, Bureh and Yoko.
By my blood, Yenga
shall not pay
taxes to the conquistador!
Beware, Sierra Leone
of your own Freetown!
The cock crowed
three times
after you sat
in your imaginary
quiet to deny Yenga
the Republican dignity.
In spite of itself, Yenga sweats.
The impossible neighbors keep
carbides in Yenga
but our politicians will not talk to them until
their French can define democracy.
In short, Sierra Leone shall never be 50
until Conakry reinvents Milton Margai.
O Yenga, when shall these
forty nights pass away?
Desert supporting desert
in the frontier of your shame.
Your beautiful oases store the veritable
bones of your courage

one child at a time.
Yenga, I'm tormented by your lugubrious drums
and I'm hopeless because my hendecasyllabic
verses have not oozed enough
the pus of my heartache.
Yenga, my Yenga, tonight I contemplate you
because I contemplate the palatine country!

AT THE GATES OF HELL I WAS TOLD

At the gates of hell I was told
That all the truths there are to be told have been told

At the gates of heaven I was told
That all the lies there are to be told have been told

Under the ember of yesterday I was told
That all the suns there are to have arisen have arisen

At the bottom of the end I was told
That all the endlessness there is to fathom has been fathomed

At the top above I was told
That all the infinite gods there are to reach have been reached

At the end of the book I was told
That all the knowledge there are to waste have been wasted

At the warmth of your love I was told
That all the temperatures there are to achieve have been achieved

WHEN THE STONE PICKED UP A LIFE

When the stone picked up a life
the earth boasted of history. Yes, a man
is capable of putting on his image all nine times
to dare the coast, jumping on rocks yards apart
and minds apart until a journey no longer becomes
necessary in all shapes or forms. In the time of no
return a stone has picked up itself to throw
a javelin right on the spot of games. In the event
of an evening wrapping around its own mind
the trick of being would be made simple.

The simple truth is that death loves
the countryside and the urban mind is never moved
to embrace opportunities that approach
like wind. Therefore, in this discourse it is inconceivable
that a mere stone would actually desire to live
beyond its silent and cold world
of rest. Some of these stones we talk about
are not really gemstones or eagerstones
or smartstones, or jetstones, or even doublestones,
always rolling on Darwin's logic.

I have a stone in my left hand
as I walk along Ceremony Avenue;
my father and his own father had a similar stone

in their left or right hands when they
walked along Ceremony Avenue;
and I hope and pray my son eventually walks Ceremony Avenue
with a stone in either hand. The citizenry
of this stone is unarguably Sierra Leonean,
with the cut of the country where the Makeni
axis and the Yonibana spread level with the Jokibu,
that begot me, O essence of my being.

Stone, suffer not this solid mind that you have given me
as I press my thumb and my little finger against
your Sierra Leonean greatness. Chances are I represent
Africa and all her proud roads, always travelling
in different directions, from the Nile to the Mile and then
to the kilometer neighbor who always wait by the door;
and with a stone in hand I dare a quantitative smile at
the world outside of Africa, outside of my immediate Sierra
and the many memories along with me
taken from the brown lips of Ceremonial Avenue.

IN SPITE OF MY RESOLVE
TO GATHER MYSELF IN THE RAIN

In spite of my resolve to gather myself in the rain
it is clear now that no one will knock on my door to peep
at me in my final room to ask whether I caught
a glance of the universal darkness outside
of my door last night.

In spite of their garrulousness
no one is ready to tender evidence that I was
seen walking into my shadow when the moon
announced its intention to rest on its universal
temper as long as the sun too will not stop
being egoistic.

In spite of my ancestral support for the tradition
that blackens my resolve to remain African
I haul away the ceremonial blood on my back
and on my chest to support a landscape
for the universal migration and scarification.

In spite of the tormenting tail of the previous day
conquered by night no one will tempt me to look
back in sorrow at the fresh grave of my mother
or my sister or the man who first
offered me water on the road from school
after the cards have offered me choices.

In spite of the gathering of the dark shoal of night
I will not taste of its water of deception
nor countenance the sticks of the striking clock
that beats into conscience the faith of another day
to be cascaded into a new garden of dawn.

In spite of the nexus between the living and the dead
no hand will receive the mirror of the ancestors
with its chronicle of how to live a life without
the sentimentalities of a god, or with its experimental
face of a broken mind dug out of the cemetery
of the treasure of the dead.

In spite of myself I will come down the air to wipe
the snout of the sweating leaf hanging over a pond, and
I will allow myself to be silent between the two
voices of the valley, and I will cast my soul
on the breasts of a corpse who has not completed her cycle.

LOOKING BLACK IN THE RAIN

Looking black in the rain
Suspects of the discourse buckle
Their shoes and don't look back
On the treasures of the corpses
Laid on the volts of the cemetery

Move on and dare the broken
Bridge and the rush of the under
Water still in image and rattling
In temperature in the shoal
Where valley and mountain meet

Don't look back on the simple road
And on the weight of the reckless
Pebble brought to life footstep
After footstep even when dead
As the stone that it is since creation

Cast your sorrows to the night
Or hang them on the sleeves of its dress
And quietly move from its moment
Move away from its terminal illness
And heed not to the song of the bat

A dead woman bleeds in your conscience
A deformed child draws swiftly to your oasis

A landscape is turning over its angry soil
A road is lost in the middle of the forest
But you must resolve to wait only in the future

The blade has torn my world apart
And my two worlds have dented the blade
Apart, apart my yesterday and my tomorrow
I run on the ropes each step going blind
Looking black in the pelting rain.

YOUR FATHER

for Barack Obama

Your father
drank the
bold waters
of the
Victoria
long ago
when it
had its
proper name.

This was
before the
British mirrored
their faces
on its glacier.

Your father
then
denied the
Victoria when
Harvard pretended
it knew
nothing about
the black
holocaust.

That same
father moderated
Harvard Harvard!

But then
the belly
of the
Livingstones kept
bringing forth
the Joyce
Careys to
walk Africa
with their
petty Johnsons.

You knew
it all,
being a
miner, and
to paraphrase
Cesar Vallejo,
you
are a
miner who,
climbing up,
you look

below Climbing
down, you
look above.

Son of
Obama you
moderated Harvard!

Son of
Barack, drink
the bold
waters of
the Mississipi,
raise your
head and
cry "Masala,
Masala" a
hundred times.

Defy the
winter that
you may
glide on
its greedy
big belly.

Do not
accept any
summer until
the battle is
won—only
then can
this century
invent its
first black
dark light!

COME WITH ME

Come with me
And follow after my following
Drink wine with me where there is no waiting
Compose yourself on the tip of a toe
And drink wine where the room is black
Never taste a glass that does not reflect your tongue
And share your hand only when it is empty
Wipe your brow when it is grey
And let *poyo* look after your conscience
Hinder not the fingers that are constant on your mouth
And *and* never talk of comparison in the house of a keg

A BRIGHT DAY OOZES OUT
OF THE MOUTH OF THE IGUANA

A bright day oozes out of the mouth of the iguana
wasting into the black hole of God; a profile is coming
out of the sweat of the sun—the day sun is separating
from the night sun and a middle staggers with bitter legs.

A war is coming out of a war staggering as a bitter leg
and the road under it sheds, tear for tear, a watery cloud
against a universal thought in the mind of a black hole
owned and owned and owned and owned and owned.

A river of war crosses over my mind and I dare to cross
over the mind of the river of war; an end of war is following
after a flash leading to the beginning of another war and
a tunnel where all of it comes to the end where there is light.

It is hard to separate moments apart from each other, apart,
by way of temperaments and by way of energy, map after map
in this universal effort to stop war; it is now clear that only
the end of war can be stopped after the iguana is coaxed.

On the rear part of a village a nagging woman carries a pot
on her head selling hot war to people constipated with peace
and it so happens that the woman who is selling war in a pot
knows nothing about her own image spread on journal covers.

If a town is going under it is fine to go to war; if a town
is going higher it is also fine to go to war, but if a town goes
neither under nor higher, anyone who goes to war to save
it saves only the self and in the end the town would shift.

In all the towns I have been to, only those with love in heart
are sure of the potentialities of war; only those who kiss
beside the candle of their skin know the energy of war
in the bones—only they know that war is inescapable.

War does not come to an end, it collapses on the knees
of another war and it is taken under the skirt of the aged,
and it is then turned into the independence of another war
and posted as a distant thought to roam in the minds of men.

THE NEWS AT 9

The news at 9
Comes up at 9
And at 9 O'clock
The news comes up
Up until 9 the peasants
Live on the morsel of 8
The laziness of 7
The brutality of 6
The hunger of 5
The theft of 4
The ignorance of 3
The roughness of 2
The paleness of 1
And then suddenly at 9
The news comes up
About the stone that was a stone

LIKE THE TREES OF THE FOREST

Like the trees of the forest
I want to stand erect and unmoved,
to shed my anger when it bothers me,
and to wave my hair to the spirit of the sky
when happiness overflows in my chlorophyll.

I want to have green clothes on among others
and stand silently in the dark woods,
and listen to the scavengers scurrying
like the tired rivers running cold
and colorless below my trunk.

I take the century by the hand and the millennium
sits on the lids of my eyes so that in looking closer
I understand the pulse of the past and in looking
into the distance I can tell the cargo of the river.

I want to stand here until I am yellow!

I HAVE SINCE STOPPED
LOVING YOU WITH MY EYES

I have since stopped loving you with my eyes
and as far as my country can let me go, I will
taste of the sweat you pour over me. This distance
between us reminds me of the yesterday we never
had in common.

I cried over my left palm after you
threw fire into my right palm. I cannot love you without
an ambidextrous desire, therefore, this painful
journey sweetens inside my chest

Behold I am left wondering whether my eyes
knows anything about love, about the flowers
of its own pupils. Could love be the tomb
of the living man? I am waiting outside
my own outside, waiting with a tomb of mind.

When Sierra Leone Was a Woman

NINE AND THE HALF

for Tatafway Tumoe

Today half of the day is sinking in the Atlantic
Outside the Rokel River
By nine and the half as half of the equal
Of love rises in the steam up above Mount Aureol.
A man stands yonder beating against his chest
Where there is no heart; love has leaked from
The drum of oil and a mess is imminent in the garden.

Cupid is passing by the night of his own body
Against the skin of green darkness,
Nine and the half between the two:
The Rokel and the Aureol;
And in the love tent of Bai Bureh I long
For love without taxes, without a little mind
But a coast of patience on the silent box of pain.
Nine and the half of me lives in a new Afrika.

A KISS COULD HAVE SAVED THE DAY

for Kula Samba

Until the hour of the revolution little
Creatures still couldn't kiss the Sierra for love.
They couldn't even stare into a mirror
Without the fear that their faces looked
Like the only man in the front pages.
They pout when they kiss in the
Cemetery of their daily lives.
Under the dark trees nobody kisses
A soul that is not a soul.

LOVE IN THE SMOKE

for Lamina Sankoh

Usually, in the streets of Freetown
After one ordinary day another follows
Until the week falls off as a weak o' can.
On this day however, I see my love in the smoke,
In blue jeans with boots full of mud.
A worm patches in my muddy heart
And writhes in the salt of the same heart
That forever waits outside the vein of my vain.

BEFORE THE NIGHT COULD BLOOM

for Sir Milton Margai

After the Provincial storm
Came the sea birds
Nestling on the muscles of the waves,
Seeking after the eye of a blind love.
In the 1800s of my Sierra the rural trees
Walked like humans
Right into the heart
Of the Pierian Spring to drink deep
from the tasty lips of the colonial goddess.

THINGS FALL APART

for Foday Sankoh

This time
It is the knife
That is falling dry
Breaking its steel
Against its own body;
Breaking a seal in the
Middle of the blood.

QUEEN OF THE LIPS

for Ella Koblo Gulama

Drawdown and look upon me against the might of my thirst.
Upon the deck in hand a window acts rudely in the wind.
Too many brooms run under the fast sky.
And I stick to the eye as your rub sticks to your soft lips.
By the candle of your hand I step into your distance,
Bringing my body and my soul by the hook of a finger.

Let our thirst halt the rude window and place
Consciousness on its pane even without taming the fender
With the universal manual of its constructor.
Drawdown and look upon the theory of love against
The night of my thirst, against the fear of Pedro Da Cintra
Who fell in love with a lion where there was no jungle.

WAS THAT WHY YOU LEFT
BY THE BACKDOOR

for Queen Yama Kapr (Yamankopra)

I read the suicide note and the murder note
You didn't write.
How you misspelled love nine hundred times.
The kettle still on top of the three stones
And the fire under
Licking the remainder of our hot water.
I will take my bath as usual besides your presence,
Dead or alive.
The wages of love is dearth.
I should have slept all last night to pull you into my dream,
Dead or alive.
Your suicide note is longer than the murder note.
Waiting in love is not the same as waiting outside love.
Once you were an oasis and all the truth
Ended under your armpits.
Now who can blame it on your Christian looks that
You cannot think chronologically?
Leap with me if you find me kind,
If you find me kind even under your suicidal skin.
I long for a tragedy like this under any circumstances.
As long as you didn't
Write both the suicide and the murder note.

THE PENSIVE MOOD OF DESIRE

for Betty Musa

The sun, she says, has gone down on her,
But many of us wonder why she has not
Turned her eyes to the hills or even to the ocean.
Between which evidence does one of her eyes show
The love she says she has lost in her other eye?
Woman, leaning on this paper wall,
The republic is searching for an army of lovers
Before the arrival of the storm with its china
Aiming at our soles.

Spy of the grammar in which of the tenses
Must love for a country be sung? Tell of the birds
Circumnavigating the under-clouds, keeping
The future under their plumages. Tell of the
Ridiculous synthesis of her desire and the man she
Chased down the cemetery in search of her own ghost,
Ghost she gave away through a greedy kiss drawn
From her reluctant lips. Tell it all, of Desire,
Her tears and of her sorrows that hold her eyes every day.

INSIDE THIS OUTSIDE

for SAJ Musa

At the height of its own abandonment, love goes
Seeking for affection between the breasts of two silences.
A rifle of love goes nosing between two Kalashnikovs.

A whole lot of yesterdays in Bunce Island keep appearing
In cannons of desire aiming for the two breasts of silence.
A rifle of love goes nosing between two Kalashnikovs

Someone is talking about the education of love, especially
After the rifles go seeking after it in places no longer called
Playgrounds; in places of the future places,
A rifle of love goes nosing between two Kalashnikovs.

UNDER THE SKIN OF YOUR KNIFE

for my side of the Atlantic

Your knife is cutting me into two sentimentalities
Ever since you wanted me to arrive at your doorstep
Holding the breath of the sea
In the singular edge of the sharpness of your love.
Daughter of the butcher where are the entrails
You promised to save for me? Here I am today
Coming a long way from a neighboring yesterday.
I cross this adjectival border on the leg of only one tongue.
Half to half I bring the harvest of your knife
Against my own journey and against the destiny
Of my journey.

I am here on account of one knife,
But there are other knives, those that chased me
On the dirt road, crossing over my head.
Where the road was tarmac I lost a shoe in the pond
Where all the consolations dropped off my shoulders.
I arrive at your doorstep not in the form you created me.
I had seven embraces between the dirt and the tarmac road.
I come alone even though I have not arrived alone.

YOUR BEAUTY MOVES ME

for the Wara Wara Hills

Your beauty moves me in a rather strange way;
In the alphabetical order of chaos.
Holding your hair, I count my fingers backwards
As the skin peels off back of where the finger nail wedges.
In matters of this nature Bassie Kondi
Peaks through the Sahara to reach my lobes,
Dropping a note just below my ego, just below…
The poet keeps telling of the fatal knife of love
When wedged between the two eyes of your heart.
I do not fathom love killing a lover
Or the knife of love cutting with hate the flesh of love.
In profile, the needles of love
Prick the body to reach the skin,
To tell of its fierce tenderness,
Of the water and fire within it.
The traffic opens an aggression,
Coaxing itself in the very weakness
Where its avenue surrenders to a little known curve.
Stop them—stop all those coming too fast
And those going away must leave the *lappa* of the image
On the body they run away from.

THE BRUTAL LANGUAGE OF LOVE

for Governor John Clarkson

Though I write to you in English
My desire is to court you in the African tongue.
I take away from the many loves of the world
To give back in like manner as spontaneously as I feel.
O stream of the polygamous rivers rushing to the sea.
For love is a cup of lake, energy of the inside.
I am in the inside dancing with those already drowned,
Dancing around the spears of flowers
That must catch their breaths forever young.
The Nile, the Victoria, and the immediate Sonfon eat me.
In that cup I am the only man who can kill myself,
The only one who can say I wish to pass over.
I am not one for resurrecting;
Therefore, it will be to love or not to love.
Let the shrine consume my passion instead of me.
A love cup full of hope
Feeding on the elixirs that feed on us.
This cup has immense hope in the instance that is me;
And you my love, coming to me in perpetual pain, you have
Neither stayed nor drafted in my continental embrace
In this tentative cup of mine.

BEFORE THE EVENING

for Sorie Forna & the Fourteen others

In the dawn of my broken heart, the sky gave me a hand
And I took it between my palms and wrapped
It around my cold body where affection
Had just passed away.

I took a pillow under the sky
And rested my head on it.
Too many other pillows stood idly around
Me, and so I took them and
Made them warm and sent them off.

The immediate urchin found one to dream on.
The retired beggar thanked his stars
When he felt one pillow below his ankle.
The vagabond un-cursed the heartless
God, who in the morning had only remembered to throw
Him a left over coin to knock himself out.

But just then, just before I noticed and took it in,
The instant serenity of it all, the old big
Hand threw in ash from the coal farm.

A JOURNEY FOR LOVE

for my late uncle, Abdulai Kargbo

A woman has come from beside me seeking a man.
A child has come from below me seeking a father.
A brother has come from above seeking a compatriot.
A sister has come from my silence seeking a voice.
A friend has come from inside of me seeking a guide.
A builder has come from without seeking a pillar.

A man has returned from being another man seeking
The ancestor who put him on his lost journey.
A parable is dangling in the clan seeking
The lips of the aged.

When finally love returns from its journey
With affection by its side, it will go directly
To the fireside to warm the thoughts
That have gone cold in its body.

TELL ME SIA LEONA, TELL ME ATHENS

for Fourah Bay College

Sia Leona, when all around you there was
Bathurst, there was the Cape Coast, there was Lagos
Reaching for your water turned to wine
What Athenian flight returned
(or not) the miners to die in the pits?

Igneous of the myth, your belly's pregnancy
The birth of the packs, were they territorial
Or Savannah?

Cottage of Freetown, of museum full of itself, which
Category demonstrates the placid self of being,
So that when I speak of you in European terms
I can forget the long arguments of the Grecian
Scroll, and just concentrate on your Afrosupremacy?

BETWEEN TWO MORTALITIES

for Aisie Talabi Lucan

A dark woman is walking up to me.
She is reading my mind in the paper
Wall of a calabash. She is walking up
To a stand of twelve candles lit in a circle
To leave her image in the circled middle.
She then turns her attention to me
Reading me like a deck of cards.
She decides on her index finger
Which she presses against
My silent skin, against the black
Beast of my skin, holding my mind
In the paper wall of a calabash.
She stares at me immortally
Through the prism of the air
That divides us, the air that falls
And rises between us.
After reading my mind she says to me,
Let there just be books.

A SONG OF NO FREE REIN

for Sierra Leoneans in the Diaspora

It took several days before she sent him a reply.
She was categorical, her hatred of automatic cars,
The robot in her legs, the persistent automation
Of life after war, the recalling of her future,
And the manner the past engages the doorway;
But what more, the anger that hastens home with her joy,
The two avenues of affection—one being a left hand
And the other being political correctness of them all;
The cupping of the birds who gather to eat the unwanted
leftovers, the secret envy of them when they take off
To ascend with Christ. For being one of two thieves,
These birds when they peck,
The firmament is their reason. Therefore, several days after
several days she found out and she replied, that she couldn't
love anyone more than she loves the birds.

115

THE ADOLESCENT WOMAN

This adolescent woman is drinking
Carlsberg under my armpit at a nightclub
Called Big Brother Big Sister.
Before now she has never gone beyond the paragraph
Of her own loneliness, nor has she ever turned herself
Into an adult woman. She is not one for a catholic eye.

I am watching her drink her Carlsberg served because
It is her wish to look into the eyes of her mother
And ask that they both danced to Steady Bongo in the rural
Urbanity of the burden of her adolescence.

She sits beside me shrinking beneath her Carlsberg
Seeking that I too have a Carlsberg to feel the same way;
To experience the fierce joy of levelling the earth.
Instantly, a dozen instances and a reluctant beam
Step out, levelling her into two sentimentalities,
All in that narrow paragraph.

AGAINST REMEMBERING

for Yulisa Amadu Maddy

Take me away from myself and separate
Me from me; ensure that I do not
Go near myself or that I do not have any cause
To talk to myself.
When I walk down the streets move me away
From the pedestrian slabs. I want to remain
Totally unconnected
To myself. I do not believe in uniforms, so I would not like
To spot myself dressed like me, nor would
I love to enter a library and encounter myself
Checking out any
Book I have written in the last twenty-something years.
Above all, people here care about me a lot, *he he he!*
And about what I think in songs for the Lady of the Sierra.
So, whenever I feel like thinking
About the rough sea, the shackles of it all,
Just keep me and myself away from me.

THESE DRUMS MUST ALWAYS BEAT

for Syl Cheney-Coker

High water, pedestrian sailing on the rhythm of foot
Against land wave, exhilarating the tune of whirlwind.
Lyric of the storm, the woman, pensive of man
Frees the season, a double echo in the year leaping.
The child, the between and the betwixt
In the embrace of the colliding storm
Must learn to be the manchild of Ngor Thara.
Set not this house on fire

Oohps! In the absence of the tribal woman
The house is on fire already, so much for the tribal woman;
The leakage, the flow of vocabularies
Of words defined in songs, evening and dawn,
The pedestrian trail of choruses,
The beating of drums for the motherland
And the flying broom in the midnight sky.

SALUTE AT THE FOOT OF UP GUN

It is through prism that one lays claim to life;
Therefore, I choose my tea cup to meet you up
at your place, plural to your singular on cruel plenitude.
This moment inexpressible of your primal moment.
Pebble by pebble, the life of death dies. Below that monster
Of the man of cowardice your French
Once trusted your English. Only when in the forum
Of the divide when you hunted La Guinea,
Brother to brother, did your Freetown ring true.

Stranger to the native tongues unable to hold your tongue
You cast the bread of sorrow two by two to local casualties.
I know you stronger by the name let out of the bag
Of school. Plural to your singular, by the hand of the river
Memory lays the foundation for the bones to stir.
The ankle runs blood to the fingers to grip.
Cannon to cannon, man to man, you wait in your waiting.
I salute you immortally in shoes old and new
At dawn the painter pauses between us two.

ONE NIGHT AT LUMELY BEACH

I remember one night in a hundred
From the backwaters of an ample Sunday
I ran across the air loving the feel of my sinking feet
In the sandy maize cold at heart befriending my soles.
It is possible to speak of Lumely beach in Atlantic terms,
In terms of an arriving vessel lit in the gloom.
It is possible to speak of this beach in terms of smoke
Oozing from the clouds with star lights seeking
The love of the patient grains.

This waterspout of the lion, from his mountain,
Length to length, the sandy exuberance of the sea
And of the elongation.
One night equals the speed of the chase and the hunger
Of the pack, the human pack in circular advent.
Lovers of the beach Lumely beckons by night and by day.
Here sensation is a climber of trees and of its breeze
Of volume. Splash of the beverage and of the booze,
The sea eats out of the sky lightening by lightening.

BUNCE ISLAND ON MY MIND

Island of my instance, healed by your own lugubrious
Syllables bring me closer to the smoke of your embrace.
Cross over my chest for the many slaves that crossed
Over yours. Twisted blood, anchor me beside M.V. Hawkins,
Beside the sadness of its captain's happiness. Within seconds
Of landing, here I am the happiness of the slave, antecedent
Of myself I sing you the shackles of the Negro spirituals.

Assembly of the circular, the famous forgetting
Of those years, the momentary busts of the grey hours—
More than enough Bunce on this Island; the cannon hearts
Their minds, those who built the noisy chains of misery.
The archaic intention, the witnessing birds viewing black
And white the invention of pain, immortal of the mortal;
Island of the servitude I love your courageous centuries.

FERRY ME ACROSS THE RIVER ROKEL

River of regency, run this cause through my veins.
Bring your creatures upon mine to achieve the lion.
Already your disposition has achieved me.
Between us two there is time immemorial
In the morning of your song compose me another
River of my two seasons, wrap around me,
Around me with the knife of your love,
And I will lie on the blunt side of your affection.

Is it possible to speak of a river
In a tense other than that in which it is running?
Or to run the cause pulling into the fatality of the sea?
Is it possible to be a riversea or a seariver
Opening up where to be narrow and narrowing down
Where to open?
Is it possible to be fresh in one's journey
And suddenly taste like salt in one's sweat?

A RIVER OF TWO SCARCIES

No longer water in their heavens,
Only the rush of their rivers went through
The weekly purgatory of the Lady's thirst—
In the little greatness of it all, the great littleness, and
A pebble of silence eating serenity by the throat.
Nickel of Caliban returned to Caliban through
The banks and the *Kaaba* marshland, also the missing
Scassos sailing to the slavers vastness, the water crying
Through the narrow bone of Kolente
Caliban and the ride, the awkward rush
To wear the insulting crown, the kingship of pain.

Regenerated Caliban in the new waters of the Scarcies,
Sailing the M.V. Miranda in common regalia, serene
On the jackass of the slavers vastness; Gangrene
of the broken nights devoid of African affection; the cyclone
Ends its putrefaction in the middle pole of the sea
Away from the great littleness and the little greatness
Of the twin sisters in the portico of the new canal.
In the influential romance of water and river
The liquid of the fresh drinks against its thirst.
Kilometer by kilometer our ladies of the North,
Side by side, sail Caliban away from the notorious cycle.

EARTHWORKS AT MASKPAIDU

A fine chaos of mind between two rivers under a river—
Puzzle of the diamond and a double barricade
Trenches raising your earth to the sky, lifting the soul
Above the spirit, the man above himself, here at Maskpaidu
Bafi and Bagbe, eye of the adventure, the romance of history
Brings lightening against the body of time. The people
Of Nimi Yema saw the lightening before the light. Stillness,
The labor confirmed even in the wasteland; easy then
To walk the town into the future tense.

Easy then to say aloud, Maskpaidu you are the locomotion.
Maskpaidu what is your name? Are you Massabendu?
Smoke of name, the little sound has taken the village
Under the foot, a road meets two rivers, crossing brown
Arriving black at Maskpaidu to write the footnote
After the note, after the smoke has arisen to spread
As ghost of page in the folio between night and day.

OLD WHARF STEPS

No songs of longer steps going taller,
Or of shorter ones receding into themselves
Compare to this brief paving in Freetown
Cascading a colony of stepsons.
Still-life flight of agony and of bitter leaves
Dying in the foot of dust.
Stair one begets stair two in longitudinal motion;
A third stair falls off to a fourth;
On it the waste of youth is a dust of wind.
And suddenly memory takes a long flight
Cascading a colony of fifth; involuntary
Pause itches under the soles, and there the dirges
Break from the image of the still-life for a breadth.
Stair six, a builder's agony resurrected.
Suddenly several stairs up and several down
On only one way, either up or down shoal is poised.
I step from myself to meet Master;
Master steps into himself to meet my kind.

LOVELESS AT LAKE SONFON

On a normal day, no one leaves home, catches a bus
To sit by a loveless lake. To lift a hammer from his heart,
A man can walk out of his people in the republic of day.
When a woman feels offended by the man she knows
As a man, she instantly divorces the world and go looking
Inside the clouds that pass over with a laboratory
Of gods for that man, who, when he was a different
Species, came to her as a moon in the dark.

I am that man by the lake fishing out the accidental gods
Falling off their test tubes. Divorced from my own rib,
I feel as vacant as a room. I am not in need of the Sonfon
Or even the little lake in my back yard. Bring me back
The woman in the first stanza, bring her straight
From the neighbor's garden, guide her to her very self
To the lake where love is less, to the lake where
My heart is wasting away, where I finally promise
To return the hour glass of the grains of affection.

AMISTAD OF THE SIERRA

On its own volition, the sea obeyed
The black faith of its pregnancy; where there
Was no Sierra, Spain bled amply under its barometer
Out of that moment came the African occasion
Spain sank away from its Amistad under the foot
Of its flag, it sank at the feet of its perambulation
Amistades Peligrosas
Too much map of freedom delayed Africa on the high seas
In America the conquistador was broken
Because of Sierra Leone
And Africa walked on water in favor of its continent
The bride of the sore throat of Spain
In his futuristic volume Alberto Comesan sang the dirge
The kilometer placard of the American adage
The simple continent of the black eye
The courage of slavery showed in the placard of the slave
And being so tagged, the hour moved its leg
Into the eyes of the brother, the embarrassed sisters
In chains in the middle of a Spanish festival
Where tomorrow's Cristina del Valle was all chorus; there,
where beneath the deck of human spite
A volcano reddened the black skin.

APPROACHING FREETOWN

Sky of bird level, sea of fish level
Oracular voyage approaching Freetown philosophically
Seeking the province, the museum of freedom
Drones in patrol in a thousand citizenry touristic of eyes
Pedro's footstool on sight, the pack too on sight
The sentimental *ashobi* in a spiritual force of gravity
The fierce transaction of citizenship on sight
The tenth acre of the land on sight
The cotton tree on sight with the lone leg of its widowhood
The De Ruyter choking beneath the abdomen
The open gates of slavery on sight in still-life
The narrow passage of freedom groans under its seams.

ANTHEM FOR THE DE RUYTER

Admiral, I salute you.
This night of the heart of this city of excavation.
History staggers on the swollen soil of the Sierra.
Under its own bottom the soul of the one buried,
When its agrarian mind, all cemeteries, shall rise
Out of an African archaeology it shall prosper as a Stone!
Stone man of my own purification
Celebrate your anniversary
Accidental avalanche of the ruined legs
Of the universal clock
This soul shall free its aura from the tinges
Of yesterday's vestiges. Up from your signature De Ruyter,
I face your own Hieroglyphics. I am forever connected to
your Eternal voyage; the swift temperament of our two
Realities, speak Africa to Africa!

MALANEH[3]

The emulous spirit in me drives me this night to mirror
My face in the sacred glass that breaks by folding its skin
On more than one soul in the Sierra Leone of my trust.
Ah! The trouble of mirroring in a sacred glass, now
The playwright of my heart begins to write his manuscript
As a mirror for my soul. *Gbash!* My memory has only
Succeeded in smashing the fiction of my looking glass.
I don't want to recall the pus in my rubber of despair but
the Perspex in my eyes calls it out into the day as I sit on
The De Ruyter Stone because my Sierra Leone is not
algebraic. It is a country made habitable by campers
Whose tracks broke the tetrameter of 1462.
I smear my virgin body with the sperm of belonging,
And I grease my heart on the hard haunch of the rock
As I hear the De Ruyter opus in the clearing of my vision;
The pastiche of Bai Bureh and the smell of the rabid
Sword. I matriculate this night on the parachute of a new
day; A reservoir of sea water dashes against my bare feet
roaring my name among this pack of Sierra Leonen poets!

---

[3] *Malaneh: Themne term for embrace*

THE MARTELLO TOWER IN THE SIERRA

A little instance interpreted itself in Sierra terms
Telling of a hill pensive of towers. The colonial fortress
repelling the arrows, chased after the vulnerable hour;
O missiles, coming across by the tick of local sorrows.

This dumb repercussion on the natives, the devised
languages, having lost their foreign grammar
Of comprehension failed to charm the black tower
Of resistance. The masters, releasing their lexicon,
Run around in the dark wind composing muteness.

SOMEONE HAD TO HAVE
LOVED MADAM YOKO

Met her against a wall staring at the front wall
Just when the world was coming to an end; sincerely
And theoretically, there had to have been a delighted man
Who decolonized himself under the pressure of this
Universal hate called love; for the sea, when it was
Never an ocean, hummed against stray ships.

This portrait has told a lie. She didn't sit all hour
To stare at a raw wall or at a color peeling
Off its vagaries. In the middle truth, after
The portrait has glided through the white
Face of her majesty's patience it shall then
Be known who it was that loved Madam to death.

THE ECONOMIC MIND OF BAI BUREH

Universal man, his own economic order,
Theory supporting warrior in the
Lynching of the tax man in his dry skin.
Taxing himself, he stood the world on its axis,
The circular thatch fronds polygamous compound
Decoder of the sea under its own theories, and
Of the land under its bottom theory, the fire blazed.

Why it was due another Caesar, this King
Did not know. Why it was him feeding
The mind of the bugler under the effort
Of his own sweat? A Savannah order
Matched with its cyclone, King against King.

Night of the conquistador! The black hand
Of betrayal gave Bai Bureh the victory of the truth!
Pink fingers of the cadaver-other wailed in their islands
And in the tender island of his own St. Helena
A wind brought the chorus of the Kasseh coast.

GBANKA OF YONI

He walked up his head into two paths
Down below his navel he was two, two in his sleep
Dreaming a dual duel. His mind was metacarpal, always
Fidgeting the stampede of his sweat. Something met
With him besides himself on the road to Kpa-Mende.

Other matters left him between himself, matters coming
Up against him on the Road from Yoni. He swore
By the evening of his name to decide between his duality,
Whether to step his left where his right had stepped out of,
Or to look ahead of his road immediately,
Against the urgent curve.

Between himself he stood with one leg raised. Toward
His pusillanimity a sword broke its demeanor and turned
Into dust of flour; two identities screwed his dour edges.

KAI LONDO OF KAILAHUN

These things when they are said belatedly of Kai Londo
Arrive at the heart with all their unsung passed

He killed another warrior close to the palm of his own hand
And sent off his head to the next pale man

These things when they are written of his sword
The plough of the oracle contends with the eternal silence

Ten hurricanes in his cyclone, the middle passage
Of his Kailahun against the waste of any savannah

Received in the fold of dawn through impossible *pehwabu*[4]
His giant silence went directly for the gargantuan emptiness

---

[4] *Pehwabu: Mende expression for a large open apartment for elderly women in-mates*

CONFESSION OF SIA LEONA'S COLONIZER

This evening of my tropical departure, I have considered
the charity of all the things I took from you,
And the chastity to reject the things I ever wanted to buy;
All those things I will deprive of my money. Do not
Think that I am under the cloud feeding on the gas
Of the dead. I do not put myself·to test. I live in
This moment only for its own gratification, for I have
Come to realize that a mortal moment is equal
To a mortal man. I pity those who celebrate anniversaries
Thinking that their celebrations recall events
In the clouds when those clouds themselves
Fold in their own fatalities with their long
Seas voyaging into eternity. What bread of anniversary
To break in the upper room of my vanity? What sea
Holds the elixir of salty water? Who can mutilate
An anger from the roughest sea to calm his own
Red Sea? Can the sage instruct me how to flee from
My own feet? How to weep in the absence of my eyes,
And how to surrender to the streams of my tears?
Who, after drinking the cup of life will escape
The cup of death? Under these restless clouds do we not
Only have one universal table to feed our guilty souls?

I.T.A. WALLACE JOHNSON, COME FORTH

In your peripheral profile a loaf of life comes with its bread
And all other particulars erect themselves a mahogany.
Under, a memorial rail brings your quick wagon alive
Honoring your cargo with a salt of heart; the brimming
Places of your erased footsteps appear on sandy prints
And now your clenched fists O Wallace, in favor
Of the Sierra, tell of your long spoon of hope at dinner,
Colonial of appetite; of the honor of the fists, the feasts,
A daiquiri telling of an African appetite.

O Wallace, you simultaneous countryman, I salute you, and
In the augmentation of your flower for my bread I kiss
Your sand true to its own mandate; because of your
Simultaneity honor comes to the dinner of the bread,
Liquid of the water, wind of the breeze, the man in our
Our own mortality. Because in your reality the life of the
Sun was longer than that of the day, you were Lazarus went
to sleep in the fertile alcove of a necessary silence.
The dawn is nigh, come forth, therefore, and be huge!

KING KAMA DUMBUYA

King, walking up to your height by the fringes of your name
The nomenclature of the country flattens in its own ball.
In regard to the fjord, the scores of the stars left the field
With you, even in the plantation of your fans, soccer is again
A slave branded in the pain of the imperial fore-chest
Of conscience, and the Leone, together with the only
Dignity of its own Stars has since returned, tear for tear,
To flood the Rokel, weakening its banks and its deposits.
King of the right and of the left leg, standing on dancing,
Your plate of name is absent on the scoreboard as your
Country's capital hazes in the college of the commonwealth.
In the vigil of our stadium we miss you in fields; between
Our eyelids, we no longer know each other as two, you,
Museum of our consolation, we speak truth to you!

YULISA

1

Yulisa!
I went searching for you among the fiercest theories of God
And I was told you left before leaving; I was told you walked
Out of your door, walking into it on the two legs
Of your standpoint; always your own;
I was told that between sunrise and sunset you built
Yourself a house and brought it down in two axe-blows;
You walked out of yourself between two centimeters
Under the humility of your own flag.

Yulisa,
Chances are you died alone between two exiles—
The instantaneous sweat of the common people
And the complacency of the country that never budged;
Volunteer of the revolution you died agriculturally
Among the controversial tenses of your restless novel
Peopled by children who like you,
Disappeared in the dust of their own heads.

Now the peasants are asking for your corpse. I do not
Have it in me. I do not have its volume in my ear.
I do not harbor its tremendous flames in my bones.
They are searching my sagacity, the peasants, seeking

The frontiers where, your immense influence lies impersonally
In my terminal silence.

2

O arts! O Amadu! Tell me where lies your Yulisa?
Shall there be no corpse for the big *berrin*? Conqueror
Of the Ides of March, a day remains implicated in your trail.
Therefore shall your profile be understood as a day
Between no day, denying the soothsayer
An incombustible flame?

Read my lips if you have walked out of your corpse and stood
Beside the right side of my left hand; if you are naked
Beside your theoretical shroud, the corpulent peasants
Are ready to bathe your body, to wash off the yellow fatigue
With sudden tears and instant sorrow, with urgent wailing
And raw gunpowder.

Ngele is waiting in the evening of her own distance,
So also is Ndaria, whose house has been taken
Over by the moon;
Fackehyeh comes upon himself in the bottle of his melancholy;
Baromi has emerged from life coming against your death with
A rope around her waist.

3

Yulisa!
You come to us in the memory of those who died in surgery.
Those courageous comrades, who, like you,
Left us before leaving.
The local hunger searches for a bookshop in Freetown, in Bo
In Makeni, in Kono, even in the slave houses, seeking to make

You a companion but only returns in the embrace of the
Undertaker. Maybe it is this reason why your corpse is not in
me, Why its volume is not in my ear, why my bones are empty
of its Tremendous flames; Even my sagacity
Goes cold in silence.

Ha! Yulisa? Yulisa! Amadu! Pat! Maddy?
Why? They who search for you have been
Looking in all the wrong places for your corpse.
There you are spread across the faces of the wretched,
The laughter of those who mourn their own demise.
You perch on the branches of their consciences,
You, yourself and your corpse,
No longer a tormented playwright!

DEATH IN THE FAMILY

For former President Ahmed Tejan Kabbah

The morning came crawling from the heath
Bringing along the backhand of the last dawn.
ATK you stand between two Freetown; the town
That is free and the town that is freeing; and the two
Thresholds, headless, return to the sentiment.

The men have finally seen reason, but by which
Time your journey had commenced; not being easy
To walk all the way to the brink, a man with a shoe
On his head is running himself to tears after the late
Night bird took away the pair of ears he never felt.

A poem built for you at any lugubrious moment has never
Stopped you from sitting arms akimbo in the children's
Playground. I remember *Lome* where you capitalized a city
And threw yourself into the arms of a warlord, forgetting
All about the instantaneous pains he had caused you.

You have gone silent with the guns and that means that
All the hurting has tasted the iodine you left behind you.
You asked us to be courageous to bid you farewell with
The rifle that you never retrieved from its place of readiness;
We will therefore torch the hay and carve you into a sky.

THE VANITY OF A LIFESPAN

To the memory of my Dad, Rev. J. E. Hallowell

Yesterday's tomorrow cannot be today
Because today is not a tomorrow.
Yesterday's tomorrow never came to be
Because it only ended up existing in man's memory.
Today's yesterday cannot be there because it ran out
Of breath and perished in the harsh lightening of the sky,
And only has its evidence in the short memory of man.
Today's tomorrow will inherit too much rough baggage
Including Man, the impossible master of the beast.
Tomorrow's today will be so remote
That archeologists will estimate
Its existence in trillions of years.
Tomorrow itself cannot be boasted about
For it may just abort.
If you were to dream up a tomorrow today, so be it;
But if I were to lose today, then what I shall step
Into cannot be a tomorrow;
Neither what I shall step out from be a yesterday.
So, if we are here today it is not because of our memory;
If we were there yesterday and miss out today,
It is not for lack of science and philosophy;
If we are not there tomorrow let us remember
That those who were not there yesterday or here today
Have their own constellations to contend with.
Today is only one of three siblings. So was yesterday;

So will be tomorrow.
The sad thing is that all three do not know each other
And will not exist all three at the same time.
All three of them exist on a twenty-four hour lifespan.
The elderly one puffs out before the middle one puffs in;
Twenty-Four hours later,
The youngest of the three puffs into the dark clock.
Yesterday appeared young at dawn
And took to midlife at noon,
Grey hairs at dusk, and puffed out at her prime.
The second and the third siblings
Always follow after this design.
Just remember those in-between whispers of the night sky:
"The earth was without form and void, and darkness was
Over the face of the deep." This is the greatest
Sorrow of all, that mankind will never know what these
three siblings suffer:
The terror of the void between them
And the void of a terror between them.

IN THE PEN DENSE

Who said you could take away
The bravery and leave us with
A mere lion, or that you could
Take away the lion and leave
Us with a mere bravery?

RE POUR BLEAK

There is the spoon in the mouth
Cold from traveling from so far
Bringing me hot food freezing with fire.

Where does this spoon come from
Ignoring all the plates waiting by me
Hungrier than I am, emptier than I am?

DEMO CRACK TRICK

He resurrected in smoke
After promising us his second coming.
We will behold him in his racist difference
Coming to feed the lion with the crack in his palms.

HALF RICKA

Of all the things you took away from me
Just return my handkerchief.
Since you left, my river
Has never stopped flowing,
And I still have the wound you left in my badge of courage.

BY BULL

Those Caucasian horns don't have any verses
Supporting the terror they brought upon my head.
Your Shakespearean slavery had no chapter in Calvary.
For the scarification on my back I continue to invoke
The bull, right here in this free town
In that of your deceptive tongue.

HINT HER LAND

They came as vociferous
Birds and perched
On the trees
We erected
With a dozen twelve hands
A dozen twelve souls
And a dozen twelve happiness.
From where they perched,
They first twitted
And then wedged
Their beaks into our skins
Deeper than we ever knew of our feelings.

WHEN SIERRA LEONE WAS A WOMAN

I

I coil under your immediate warmth
pulling myself toward your acceptance;
against my animal beatitude, I come,
leaving that bloody essence
in my personal beast of a nation;
your portrait with its own song
has taken me up above limitless clouds
to give my heart to your expanse
      to give my heart to the paper work of your love;
here is my everyday essence in a green bowl
instead of the calabash already full of cola nuts;
here is to my republican indices
and my traditional myth. The men outside
are slapping their mosquito thighs and saying
to one another, "When Sierra Leone was a woman..."

II

Country, my love for you is horizontal
in a vertical sense. Suffer me always the legend
in my supplication speaking of breasts full of milk
and the tumblers rolling beneath the eaves where
the cloying is receiving droplets

151

of approval in water format,
    and I, in liquid hope
stretch out the hands of the child without
a mind of judgment but with a smile favoring
the face of bonding. The women, clutching
their winnowers, recall:
"Ah, when Sierra Leone was a woman…"

III

In whose belly I shall die I do not know
Yet I think of you, Freetown and of your Sierra.
I shall like to die in your belly freely
        Dead six feet four below the final breath
that *thins* the leaf and paints it brown;
mine is no ample love for you
but of a homeless thought.
I love you anyway in a rather exilic manner
when there is a desert and you come
falling on yourself
your road, when it is coming
down and you walking up
waking the atom in the stone, I find time
to wonder why people say,
"When Sierra Leone was a woman…"

Printed in the United States
By Bookmasters